DO NOT REMOVE
CARDS FROM POCKET

SPACE PROBES TO THE PLANETS

Fay Robinson

ALBERT WHITMAN & COMPANY / Morton Grove, Illinois

For my father. F.R.

Thanks to April Whitt, Astronomer,
the Adler Planetarium, Chicago, Illinois

CREDITS:
Photos and artwork from NASA: cover, pp. 1, 3, 6, 7,
8, 9, 10, 11, 12, 13, 15, 16, 17, 18-19, 20, 21, 22, 24, 25,
26, 28, 29, 31, 32
U.S. Geological Survey, Flagstaff, AZ.: p. 14
JPL/NASA: p. 23
Illustrations and diagrams by Bruce Kerr: pp. 4-5, 16,
26, 27

Library of Congress Cataloging-in-Publication Data

Robinson, Fay.
  Space probes to the planets / Fay Robinson.
    p.   cm.
  Summary: Text and photos present the information
collected by spacecraft with no people on them, known
as space probes, which have penetrated the areas
around planets as far away as Neptune.
  ISBN 0-8075-7548-8
  1. Planets—Juvenile literature. [1. Planets. 2. Space
probes.] I. Title.
QB602.R62   1993   92-10792
523.4—dc20   CIP
                                              AC

Text © 1993 by Fay Robinson.
Illustrations © 1993 by Albert Whitman & Company.
Published in 1993 by Albert Whitman & Company,
6340 Oakton Street, Morton Grove, Illinois 60053.
Published simultaneously in Canada by
General Publishing, Limited, Toronto.
All rights reserved. Printed in U.S.A.
10 9 8 7 6 5 4 3 2 1

The text for this book is set in Stone Sans-Semibold.
The illustrations are in watercolor and gouache.
The book design is by Susan B. Cohn.

Have you ever wanted to visit another planet? Ever since the
planets were discovered, people have dreamed of visiting them.
But the planets are all very hot or very cold, and very far away.
Until scientists learn more, a trip to explore them would be unsafe.

In the meantime we've learned a lot about the planets, partly
because of space probes. Space probes are spacecraft with no
people on them. With the help of computers and radio signals,
they can travel to the planets by themselves.

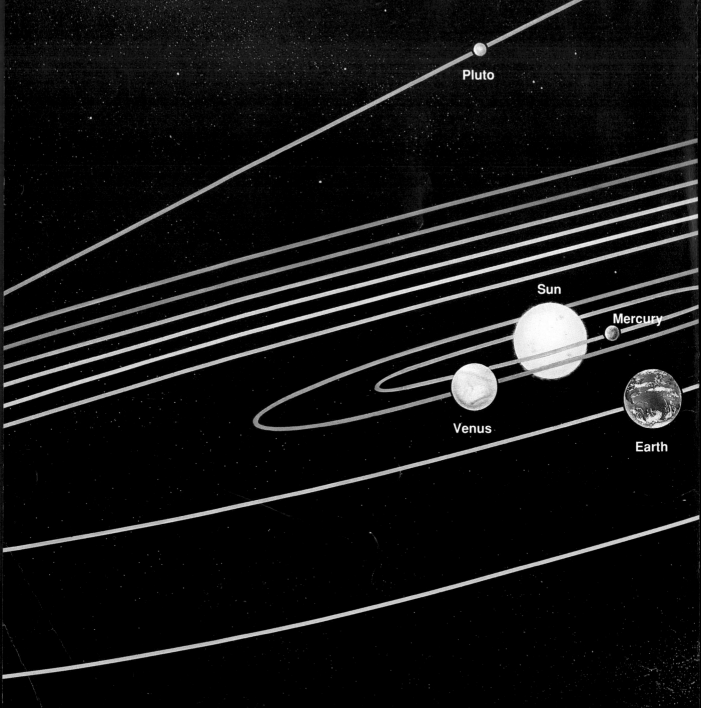

Earth, the planet we live on, is one of nine planets that circle the sun. The nine planets are Mercury, Venus, Earth, Mars, Jupiter, Saturn, Uranus, Neptune, and Pluto. Most of the planets have moons that travel with them. Rocky objects called meteoroids and asteroids circle the sun between the planets. The sun and all the planets and objects that circle it are called the solar system.

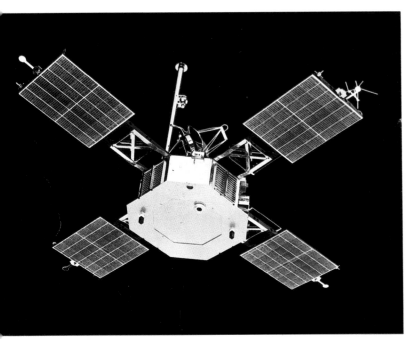

Mariner 5

Viking Lander

Voyager

Space probes have flown close to all the planets except Pluto, and some have landed on Venus and Mars. The planets are all very far away from Earth—so far that it took three months for space probes to get to the closest planet, and twelve years to get to the farthest.

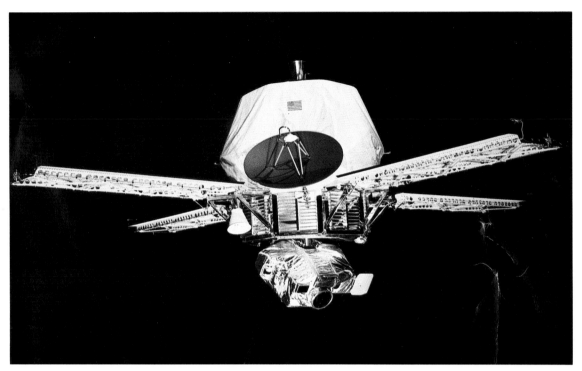

Mariner 9

The space probes collected lots of information about each planet's atmosphere, temperatures, moons, and more. But the most exciting information came from pictures the space probes took. When the space probes got up close to the planets, scientists discovered some incredible things.

Pioneer Orbiter

Craters and ridges on Mercury

MERCURY, the planet closest to the sun, is covered with round holes called craters. Pictures from a space probe showed that Mercury has more craters for its size than any other planet. The craters were formed when millions of big rocks, or meteorites, crashed into Mercury long ago.

Mercury also has long ridges that look a little like wrinkles. Scientists think Mercury shrank after it was formed. The surface wrinkled the same way grapes wrinkle as they dry and shrink to become raisins.

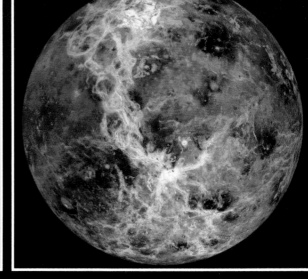

Venus with its cloud cover   *Venus beneath its cloud cover*

VENUS, the second planet from the sun, is wrapped in swirling clouds. Even though Venus is not the closest planet to the sun, it is the hottest. Its clouds are very thick and heavy, so they act like a blanket to trap heat. Powerful lightning bolts flash through the clouds all the time.

Venus is so hot that when space probes landed on its surface, their parts melted. In order to learn more about Venus without losing any more space probes, scientists developed a way to get pictures through the clouds. These pictures show spots, cracks, and places where melted rock has pushed through the surface to make odd shapes.

EARTH is the third planet from the sun and the planet we live on. From far away in space, we can see blue oceans, brown land, and white clouds. Close-up pictures show our forests, mountains, rivers, and seas.

Earth is the only planet with lots of water. Since plants and animals need water to live, Earth is the only planet with plant and animal life. Scientists think it is the only planet in our solar system with *any* kind of life. Earth also has the perfect temperature for people—the other planets would be too hot or cold for us unless we wore special space suits.

MARS, the fourth planet from the sun, is nicknamed the Red
Planet because of its red-orange color.

As space probes approached Mars, scientists saw grooves that looked like dried riverbeds. They decided Mars once had rivers like those we have on Earth. They wondered, if there was once water on Mars, were there living creatures, too?

When two space probes landed on Mars' surface, scientists hoped their close-up pictures would show signs of life. But all they showed was a rocky surface under a pink sky.

Top: *Grooves on Mars' surface*
Bottom: *Mars seen from a space probe on its surface*

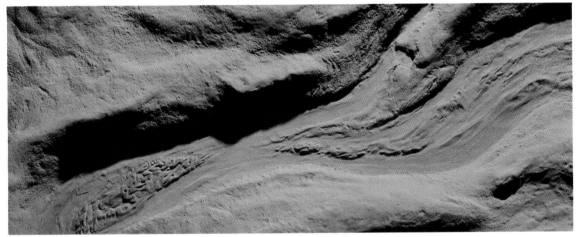

JUPITER is the fifth planet from the sun and the largest. If you could put eleven Earths side by side, they would not quite reach through Jupiter's middle.

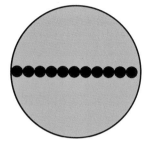

Jupiter has enormous windstorms. One storm, called the Great Red Spot, is a hurricane three times larger than the planet Earth.

Scientists knew Jupiter was colorful, but when space probes took these pictures, scientists were amazed. No one knew that the colors made such beautiful designs.

The Great Red Spot

The colors on Jupiter come from different kinds of clouds. The clouds are striped because Jupiter spins very quickly—so quickly that the clouds are stretched into bands. All the planets spin, but Jupiter spins faster than any other.

SATURN, the sixth planet from the sun, is surrounded by spectacular rings. Pictures from the space probes showed thousands of thin rings around Saturn, each traveling in its own path. There are three other planets with rings, but no planet has as many as Saturn.

Above: *Saturn's rings and their shadows*
Left: *Saturn's rings (Scientists added colors for clarification)*

The rings are made of pieces of ice and icy rock. Most pieces are the size of an ice cube, but some are as small as a grain of sand, and some are as large as a house. The space probes also found that Saturn has at least eighteen moons—more than any other planet.

	Number of Moons	*Number of Rings*
Mercury	0	0
Venus	0	0
Earth	1	0
Mars	2	0
Jupiter	16	1
Saturn	at least 18	thousands
Uranus	15	11
Neptune	8	3
Pluto	1	0

URANUS, the seventh planet from the sun, has a hazy glow. When pictures of Uranus started coming in from a space probe, scientists were disappointed that there were no spots, stripes, or designs. One scientist thought Uranus looked like a "fuzzy blue tennis ball."

Uranus has rings that go up and over it instead of around its middle. This is because Uranus is tipped on its side. Some scientists think a planet or other huge object may have bumped into Uranus and knocked it over.

Uranus and its rings

The Great Dark Spot and Scooter

NEPTUNE, the eighth planet from the sun, is deep blue. A space probe took pictures of white clouds that streaked very quickly around the planet. One cloud moved so fast that scientists called it Scooter. Scientists learned that Neptune's strong winds push some clouds to speeds of seven hundred miles per hour—faster than an airplane.

Neptune also has huge storms like those on Jupiter. Scientists named the biggest one the Great Dark Spot. This storm is as large as the planet Earth. Some scientists think there may be pure diamond at Neptune's center, created by a special combination of heat, pressure, and gases.

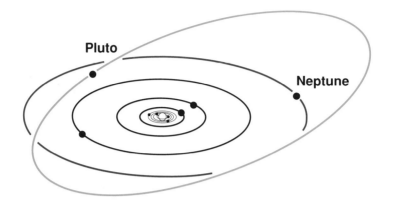

PLUTO is the ninth planet from the sun most of the time, but right now it is closer to the sun than Neptune. This is because Pluto's trip around the sun follows an unusual path. After the year 1999, Pluto will again be the farthest planet.

Pluto is the only planet that no space probe has explored. Scientists will learn much more when a space probe gets close, but for now they have pictures taken from a telescope in space.

Pluto and its moon

Painting of what Pluto and its moon might look like

Pluto has a moon that is half its size, so some scientists think of Pluto as a double planet. It is the smallest planet and is so far away from the sun that it is probably frozen solid.

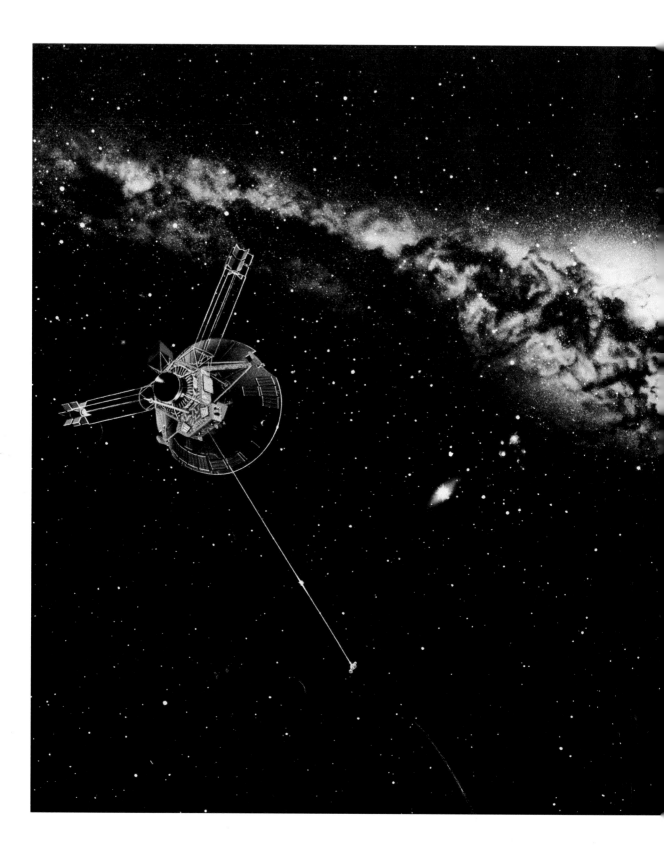

What happened to the space probes that traveled to the planets? They stayed in space. The probes that landed on Mars and Venus are still there. The probes that circled Mars, Venus, and Mercury are still circling. And the probes that flew past the other planets are now flying farther and farther into space.

Someday, they may fly into other solar systems. They will be too far away to send photographs or other information by then. But if there are any living beings who come across those space probes, they may be able to learn about us. Two of the space probes carry a record that plays sounds from Earth—the voices of people saying hello in many different languages, the sounds of whales, frogs, heartbeats, and rainstorms.

Meanwhile, scientists are studying the information the space probes collected. They are sending other space probes to the planets to learn more. Someday soon, we may be able to visit another planet. We will need all the information the space probes can give us.

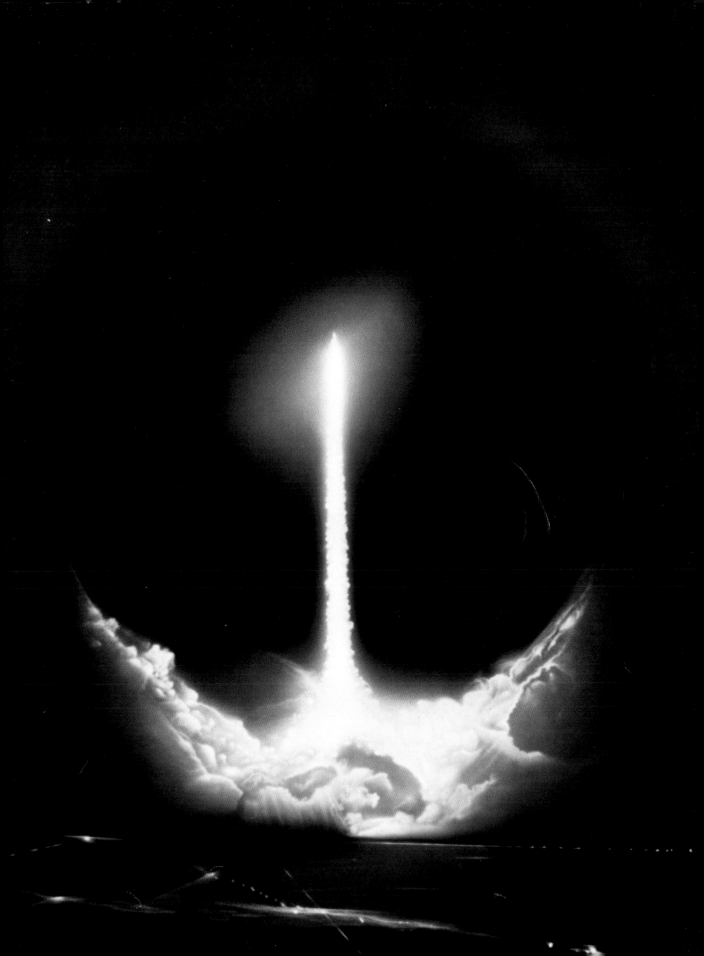

More About Space Probes

How do space probes get to the planets?

Space probes are sent into space either by rockets or by space shuttles. These launch vehicles carry the space probes through the Earth's atmosphere, then boost them on their paths to the planets.

How do space probes "know" what to do?

Space probes are run by computers. The computers act like brains to receive instructions from scientists at computers on Earth.

How do scientists get the pictures from the space probes?

The space probes carry special cameras. These cameras don't use film like cameras you may have. Instead, they send pictures down to computers on Earth through electrical signals—similar to the way television pictures are sent through the air to your TV.

Scientists then turn the pictures on the computer screens into photographs.